Richard Raskin

COLOR

An Outline of Terms and Concepts

AARHUS UNIVERSITY PRESS
1986

AARHUS UNIVERSITY PRESS
Aarhus University
DK-8000 Aarhus C
Tel. 06 19 70 33

This publication was supported by a grant
from Aarhus University's Research Foundation.

Front cover left: Newton's color circle in OPTICK, 1666 (color added).
Front cover right: Goethe's first diagram in his THEORY OF COLOR, 1810.
Back cover: Athanacius Kircher, ARS MAGNA LVCIS ET VMBRAE, 1646.

JOHANNES ITTEN'S TWELVE-HUE COLOR CIRCLE

The twelve hues can be listed as follows in their 'clockwise' position on the color circle:

12. yellow
 1. yellow-orange
 2. orange
 3. red-orange
 4. red
 5. red-violet

 6. violet
 7. blue-violet
 8. blue
 9. blue-green
10. green
11. yellow-green

While reading the definitions of PRIMARY, SECONDARY, TERTIARY and COMPLEMENTARY COLORS in subsequent sections of this book, the reader may wish to refer repeatedly to this illustration, which is based on a figure in KUNST DER FARBE, © 1961 and 1970 by Otto Maier Verlag, Ravensburg.

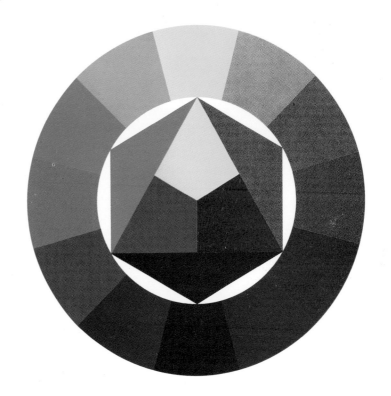

INTRODUCTION

****

Students and teachers of art, as well as anyone else who is interested in painting, may find this booklet useful as an overview of basic color terms and concepts. In mapping out in outline form what I think is most essential in this context, I have drawn on a number of books on the subject, citing 'standard' formulations as well as expressions of individual points of view, clearly labeled as such (for example, "Arnheim's contention").

Knowing very little about the science of optics and the physiology of vision, I thought it wise to leave those subjects to writers who can deal with them competently. The reader should therefore not expect to find here a discussion of the wavelengths of the various hues, the Munsell or Ostwald color systems, or the ways in which the eye functions when perceiving light and color.

What the reader _can_ expect to find is an attempt to present the basics as clearly and concisely as possible, without the use of 'padding'. In order to keep the cost of this booklet within reasonable limits, few color illustrations have been used. In accordance with the wisdom of turning losses into gains, the reader is asked to make up for the lack of color plates by illustrating portions of this booklet himself or herself--which is probably the best way to learn the material in any event.

Richard Raskin
Aarhus
June-July 1986

TABLE OF CONTENTS

* *

COLOR ILLUSTRATIONS

saturation

low
saturation

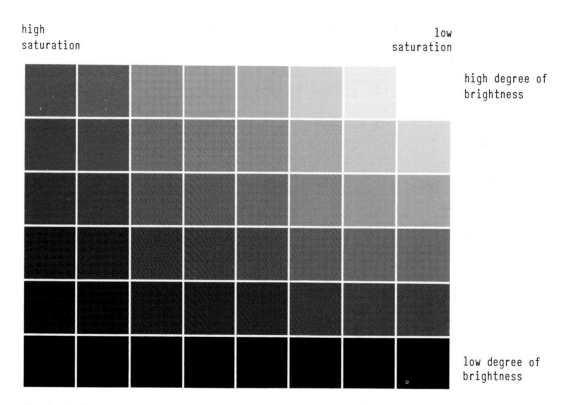

high degree of
brightness

low degree of
brightness

Chart showing degrees of saturation and brightness for a single hue.

THREE ATTRIBUTES OF COLOR SENSATION : HUE, SATURATION AND BRIGHTNESS
****

CHROMATICITY	HUE	Graves: "the quality or characteristic by which we distinguish one color from another: a red from a yellow or a green from a purple." Science of Color: "the attribute most commonly associated with the wavelength... of the stimulus." Bustanoby: "often used as a synonym for the word 'color'." An achromatic color (white, gray, black) is defined as a color without hue.
	SATURATION or CHROMA	Agoston: "the apparent concentration of hue." Graves: "Chroma is the strength, intensity, or purity of a color." Science of color: "the degree to which a chromatic color sensation differs from an achromatic color sensation of the same brightness." Hansen: saturation varies inversely with the amount of white contained in the color. Adding white to a color decreases its saturation and produces a TINT.
BRILLIANCE	BRIGHTNESS or VALUE	Birren: "the lightness or darkness of a color as compared with the steps of a gray scale." Brightness varies inversely with the amount of black contained in the color. Adding black to a color decreases its brightness and produces a SHADE.

NB. Adding gray (black and white) to a color lowers both saturation and brightness and produces a TONE.

ADDITIVE and SUBTRACTIVE COLOR MIXTURE and PRIMARY COLORS
****

ADDITIVE MIXTURE	SUBTRACTIVE MIXTURE
Examples: stage lights of different colors simultaneously focused on the same object (superposition); tiny blue, green and red dots on a TV screen producing the full range of color sensation (partitive mixing).	Examples: the mixing of dyes and paints; passing light through a series of colored filters.
"The more lights that are added, the brighter is the net effect" (Williamson & Cummins).	"the more colors that are mixed together the dimmer becomes the surface" (Williamson & Cummins).
additive primaries: red, green and blue	subtractive primaries: red, yellow and blue, often specified as magenta, yellow and cyan.
mixing the primaries in the proper proportions results in white	mixing the primaries in the proper proportions results in black
red + green = yellow	red + green = gray
"the gamut of colors produced by (the primaries) includes all hues" (Agoston), and no combination of any two of the primaries matches the third; the subtractive primaries are the complementaries of the additive primaries.	
the primaries and their properties were first described in 1802 by Thomas Young	the primaries and their properties were first described in 1756 by Le Blon

NB. Some writers refer to the following as the six PSYCHOLOGICAL PRIMARIES: red, yellow, green, blue, black and white.

SECONDARY AND TERTIARY COLORS (subtractive context)
****

produced by combining	SECONDARY	TERTIARY	
produced by combining	two primary colors; some writers specify 'in equal parts' (Chevreul)	"any primary with either of its adjacent secondaries" (Goldstein)	
colors	orange green violet	yellow-orange red-orange red-violet	blue-violet blue-green yellow-green

NB. In an additive context, the secondaries are: yellow (red + green), cyan and magenta.

COMPLEMENTARY COLORS
****

COMPLEMENTARY COLORS can be defined as two colors which complete or 'complement' each other in the sense that any primary not included in one of them is found in or coincides with the other. Consequently, mixing complementary colors necessarily involves the mixing of all three primary colors, and a balanced mixture of complementaries is achromatic (white light in the case of additive mixture by superposition, and dark gray or black when colorants are subtractively blended). Complementary pairs:

additive context	
primaries	secondaries
RED	GREEN-BLUE (CYAN)
BLUE	YELLOW
GREEN	BLUE-RED (MAGENTA)

subtractive context			
primaries	secondaries	tertiaries	
RED	GREEN	YELLOW-ORANGE	BLUE-VIOLET
BLUE	ORANGE	YELLOW-GREEN	RED-VIOLET
YELLOW	VIOLET	RED-ORANGE	BLUE-GREEN

Some other characteristics of subtractive complementaries: a) complementaries are situated diametrically opposite each other on a color circle; b) adding a small amount of its complementary to a color reduces the color's brightness; c) the complement of a primary color is necessarily a secondary color (i.e. a mixture of the two other primaries), while the complement of a tertiary color is always another tertiary; d) juxtaposing complementaries heightens the intensity of both; e) "in complementary colours the warmer the orange the colder its complementary blue..." (Hiler).

SUCCESSIVE CONTRAST
****

"The successive contrast of colours includes all the phenomena which are observed when the eyes, having looked at one or more coloured objects for a certain length of time, perceive, upon turning them away, images of these objects, having the colour complementary to that which belongs to each of them" (Chevreul).

Successive contrast involves the production of an after-image in colors complementary to those which were stared at during the initial phase of the process.

Goethe considered these phenomena to be of the greatest importance "since they direct our attention to the laws of vision," by which he meant: "They show that the eye especially demands completeness and seeks to eke out the color wheel in itself." In this respect, successive contrast was the very basis for Goethe's conception of harmony, which he saw as the fulfillment of the eye's wish for color combinations which--as complementaries do by definition--embrace the entire spectrum.

SUCCESSIVE CONTRAST. Stare at the red square in a strong light for twenty seconds. Then look at the inner white square in the figure at the right, and observe the after-image of a green square on a violet ground. This is one of the examples Chevreul used to illustrate successive contrast.

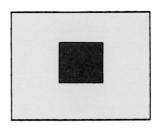
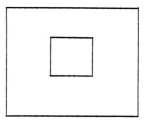

SIMULTANEOUS CONTRAST

BRIGHTNESS CONTRAST or CONTRAST OF TONE: This refers to the 'fluting' effect that can be observed when stripes of different values of the same hue, or of gray, are juxtaposed. Here, for example, the stripe in the middle appears to be darker at the edge meeting the lighter stripe, and lighter along the edge adjacent to the darker one, despite the fact that it is perfectly uniform in value.

CONTRAST OF COLOR: Chevreul's general formula for simultaneous contrast reads as follows: "In the case where the eye sees at the same time two contiguous colors, they will appear as dissimilar as possible, both in their optical composition and in the height of their tone." Specifically with regard to the simultaneous contrast of color, the following are among the variants or consequences of this law:

a) "Colorants of similar hue appear more like each other's complementary hue when juxtaposed" (Graves). Consequently, "When we place near orange a scarlet-red..., we see that the red acquires a purple, and the orange a yellow tint" (Chevreul). In other words, the orange 'pulls' the red toward blue, and the red 'pulls' the orange toward green.

b) When a primary and a secondary color with one common element are juxtaposed--for example, green and blue--"we see that by their reciprocal influence they lose more or less of the color which is common to both" (Chevreul), in this case the "green loses some blue and appears yellower; the blue becomes redder, differing as much as possible from green." Similarly, when two secondary colors with a common element are juxtaposed, both colors are pulled away from the color they share. When green and orange are placed side by side, "the orange will appear redder and the green bluer" (Chevreul).

c) "A gray tends to appear like the complementary of its background" (Graves). For example, when gray is placed on a green background, "the gray appears inclining to red by receiving the influence of the complementary green" (Chevreul).

d) A color placed on a white background tends to appear "brighter and deeper," and to color the surrounding space faintly with its complement (Chevreul).

e) A color placed on a black background tends to appear lighter or brighter and to pull the black toward its complement. Thus when green is placed on black: "The complementary of green (red), uniting with the black, the black appears more violet or reddish. The green inclines slightly to yellow" (Chevreul).

f) When complementaries are juxtaposed, no change of hue occurs, but both colors appear more intense.

Carpenter: "The opposite effect from simultaneous contrast is termed a 'spreading effect'. When colors thread through each other rather than being juxtaposed in relatively large areas, the sensation of one spreads over another, a light color making its surroundings lighter, a warm color making its surroundings warmer, and so on."

Ehrenzweig: "The spreading effect is the very opposite of colour interaction. Colour interaction heightens the difference between two colours and pushes them towards the complementaries... If a colour is inhibited by strong composition (line, tonal contrast, etc.) it will instead tend to spread. Instead of enhancing colour contrast--as in colour interaction--it will tinge any suitable area with its own hue. Spreading seems to be capable of affecting an area wider than that usually affected by colour interaction, as though a colour which was able to break out from its prison had the strength to spread almost over the entire picture plane, checked only by the opposing action of colour interaction."

Examples of simultaneous contrast and of spreading will be found on pages 14 and 26, respectively.

"Broadly speaking, a strong composition inhibits the mutual enhancement of colour surfaces (simultaneous colour contrast, colour interaction); conversely the mutual enhancement of colours tends to weaken form and tonal contrasts, the relationship between figure and ground and illusions of depth produced by perspective. Form and colour belong to different levels of aesthetic experience. As Gombrich has pointed out, the experience of colour stimulates deeper levels of the mind. This is demonstrated by experiments with mescaline, under the influence of which the precise outlines of objects become uncertain and ready to intermingle freely with little regard to formal appearances; on the other hand colour becomes greatly enhanced, tends to detach itself from the solid objects and assumes an independent existence of its own.

Form is altogether more rational. In teaching draughtsmanship the control of line is more amenable to intellectual mastery. In accordance with the more intellectual climate now obtaining in art schools some intellectual control of colour is taught, but no systematic study of the fundamental conflict between form and colour is attempted...

...A strong shape will tend to stand out as a figure against an indistinct ground. The stronger the figure effect the weaker will be the colour interaction between figure and ground. For the same reason a strong space illusion created by perspective and other formal means, such as the overlapping of shapes, will also diminish the colour interaction within the picture.

...Strong colour interaction tends to make sharp outlines seem much softer than they are...

We have to understand that in the conflict between strong colour and strong form each adversary grows in stature and power through their mutual confrontation."

SIMULTANEOUS CONTRAST OF COLOR. Although the two red rectangles are identical in color, the one on the red-violet background looks considerably more orange than does the one on the yellow background, since in each case, the red is 'pulled' toward the complementary of the surrounding color. (See pp. 11-12 above.)

SEVEN TYPES OF HARMONY
****

types and definitions	examples	(upper case for KEY hues)	
ANALOGOUS HARMONY (3 colors): combining a color with those immediately adjacent to it, on both sides, on a color circle. "With analogous color schemes, effects are generally best when the key hue is a primary or a secondary" (Birren).	red violet +	RED +	red orange
	red orange +	ORANGE +	yellow orange
	yellow orange +	YELLOW +	yellow green
	yellow green +	GREEN +	blue green
	blue green +	BLUE +	blue violet
	blue violet +	VIOLET +	red violet
COMPLEMENTARY HARMONY (2 colors): combining a color with its complementary.		red +	green
		red orange +	blue green
		orange +	blue
		yellow orange +	blue violet
		yellow +	violet
		yellow green +	red violet
SPLIT COMPLEMENTARY (3 colors): combining a color with those immediately adjacent to and on both sides of its complementary.	blue green +	RED	+ yellow green
	blue +	RED ORANGE	+ green
	blue violet +	ORANGE	+ blue green
	violet +	YELLOW ORANGE	+ blue
	red violet +	YELLOW	+ blue violet
	red +	YELLOW GREEN	+ violet
	red orange +	GREEN	+ red violet
	orange +	BLUE GREEN	+ red
	yellow orange +	BLUE	+ red orange
	yellow +	BLUE VIOLET	+ orange
	yellow green +	VIOLET	+ yellow orange
	green +	RED VIOLET	+ yellow

DOUBLE SPLIT COMPLEMENTARY (4 colors): With a given pair of complementaries as a point of reference, a combination is made of the colors immediately adjacent to and on both sides of each of the complementaries.			
red violet	+ red orange	+ blue green	+ yellow green
red	+ orange	+ blue	+ green
red orange	+ yellow orange	+ blue violet	+ blue green
orange	+ yellow	+ violet	+ blue
yellow orange	+ yellow green	+ red violet	+ blue violet
yellow	+ green	+ red	+ violet

TRIADIC (3 colors): combining three colors equidistant from each other on the color circle (for example, every fourth color on a 12-hue color circle).		
red	+ yellow	+ blue
red orange	+ blue violet	+ yellow green
orange	+ violet	+ green
yellow orange	+ red violet	+ blue green

QUADRATIC (4 colors): combining four colors equidistant from each other on the color circle (for example, every third color, starting anywhere on a 12-hue color circle).			
red	+ yellow orange	+ green	+ blue violet
red orange	+ yellow	+ blue green	+ violet
orange	+ yellow green	+ blue	+ red violet

HARMONY OF SCALE or MONOCHROMATIC HARMONY: "strongly different values of a single hue are combined" (Birren); "an agreeable sensation, especially if the tones are at equal intervals and sufficiently numerous" (Chevreul).

THREE CONCEPTIONS OF HARMONY
****

GOETHE : HARMONY AS COMPLETENESS

For Goethe, successive contrast was the key to understanding the nature of harmony. He wrote, in §805-807 of his FARBENLEHRE: "When the eye sees a color it is immediately excited, and it is its nature, spontaneously and of necessity, at once to produce another, which with the original color comprehends the whole chromatic scale. A single color excites, by a specific sensation, the tendency to universality. To experience this completeness, to satisfy itself, the eye seeks for a colorless space next every hue in order to produce the complemental hue upon it. In this resides the fundamental law of all harmony of colors..."

OSTWALD : HARMONY AS MEASURED INTERVAL

"The main proposition of color harmony takes this form: those colors are harmonious, or belong together, whose attributes are definitely and simply related to each other" (cited by Jacobson). One such definite and simple relationship can be seen in chords of three or more colors chosen according to the 'principle of equal-interval repetition,' whereby--for example--the colors in the chord represent every third gradation of brightness within a given hue at the same level of saturation. This measured relationship with regard to gradations of brightness or saturation, or some other regularity of interval between the colors in the chord, constitutes a chromatic equivalent to meter or rhythm.

ARNHEIM : HARMONY AS STASIS

Formulating a "fundamental objection to the principle on which the rules of color harmony are based," Arnheim wrote: "This principle conceives of a color composition as a whole in which everything fits everything. All local relations between neighbors show the same pleasant conformity. Obviously this is the most primitive kind of harmony, suitable at best for the so-called color schemes of clothing or rooms, although there seems to be no reason why even a dress or a bedroom should cling to a noncommittal homogeneity of color rather than setting accents, creating centers of attention, separating elements by contrast. Certainly a work of art based on such a principle could describe nothing but a world of absolute peace, devoid of action, expressing only a static over-all mood. It would represent that state of deadly serenity at which, to use the language of the physicist, entropy approaches a maximum."

****

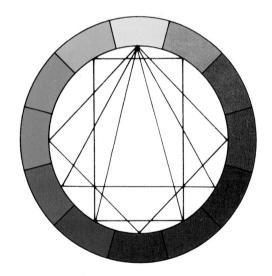

Itten's illustration of various harmonies. Any one geometric figure can be rotated to any position within the 12-hue color circle and the colors indicated by the figure's corners will constitute a harmony.

Here color has been added to the illustration appearing in Itten's KUNST DER FARBE ©1961 and 1970 by Otto Maier Verlag, Ravensburg.

COOL AND WARM COLORS and their SPATIAL PROPERTIES
****

	COOL	WARM
definition	"any hues in which blue predominates" (Bustanoby)	"any hues in which red-orange predominates" (Bustanoby)
affective properties	passive, calming (Birren)	active, exciting (Birren)
	"The warm colors, yellow, orange and red, are positive and aggressive, restless, or stimulating, as compared to the cool violets, blues and greens, which are negative, aloof and retiring, tranquil and serene" (Graves). See also the properties ascribed to individual colors (pp. 20-22 below).	
Arnheim's contention	"The terms 'warm' and 'cold' have little reference to pure hues... The two terms seem to acquire their characteristic meaning when they refer to the deviation of a given color in the direction of another color. A bluish yellow or red tends to look cold, and so does a yellowish red or blue. On the contrary, a reddish yellow or blue seems warm. My contention is that not the main color but the color of the slight deviation from it determines the effect... It is only when a color produces a dynamic tension by leaning toward another color that it reveals its expressive characteristics."	
spatial properties: standard claims	pull backwards (Itten); recede, give an illusion of being relatively distant (Bustanoby)	push forward (Itten); give an illusion of being relatively near (Bustanoby)
	"Warm colors in the foreground and cool ones in the background strengthen the effect of depth and space. If the warmest red is in the background and the coolest blue in the foreground, the effect of space is spoiled; the color perspective contradicts the linear perspective" (Dantzig).	
Ruskin's challenge	"It is a favourite dogma among modern writers on colour that 'warm colours' (reds and yellows) 'approach' or express nearness, and 'cold colours' (blue and grey) 'retire' or express distance. So far is this from being the case, that no expression of distance in the world is so great as that of the gold and orange in twilight sky. Colours, as such, are ABSOLUTELY inexpressive respecting distance. It is their quality (as depth, delicacy, etc.) which expresses distance, not their tint" (THE ELEMENTS OF DRAWING, p. 177).	

AFFECTIVE AND SYMBOLIC PROPERTIES OF INDIVIDUAL COLORS
****

Wittgenstein argued: "...I think that it is worthless and of no use whatsoever for the understanding of painting to speak of the characteristics of the individual colors. When we do it, we are really only thinking of special uses. That green as the colour of a tablecloth has this, red that effect, does not allow us to draw any conclusions as to their effect in a picture" (§213). In another context, Wittgenstein evoked the same fallacy in the following way: "Imagine someone pointing to a place in the iris of a Rembrandt eye and saying: 'The walls in my room should be painted this colour'" (I, §58). The following is a sampling of what various commentators have claimed, as well as Roman Catholic and heraldic color symbolism.

	positive associations	negative associations	writer	Catholic	heraldic
RED	gravity, dignity, grace, attractiveness		Goethe	charity, generous sacrifice, martyrdom	courage, zeal
	passionate physical love	war, demonic	Itten		
	courage, virility, sex	rage, strife, danger	Graves		
	passionate, exciting, fervid, active	rage, rapacity, fierceness, blood	Birren		
	vitality, action, warmth, joy, pleasure	danger, cruelty, anger, lust, torture, hatred, destruction	Bustanoby		
	"Yellow and red... are the colors of the material, the near, the full blooded. Red is the characteristic color of sexuality. Yellow and red are popular colors, the colors of the crowd, of children, of women and of savages... Red and yellow... belong to the foreground even in respect of social life; the noisy hearty market-days and holidays."		Spengler		
ORANGE	warmth, gladness (red-yellow)		Goethe		strength, endurance
	sunlike radiance in the material sphere, warm, active energy; festive	proud, outer splendour	Itten		

	positive associations	negative associations	writer	Catholic	heraldic
ORANGE cont.	jovial, lively, energetic, forceful, hilarity, exuberance, satiety		Birren		
	warm, invigorating, vitality, strength				
YELLOW	in pure and bright state: warm, agreeable, serene, noble	when greenish: very disagreeable and unpleasant	Goethe		(gold) honor loyalty
	understanding, insight; cheerful, radiant	envy, treachery, falsehood, doubt, confusion	Itten		
	"Bright, clear yellow is emblematic of the sun and is cheerful, gay and lively."	"The darker... and greenish yellows are the most unpopular of all colors... associated with sickness and disease, indecency, cowardice, jealousy, envy, deceit, and treachery."	Graves		
	"cheerful brightening color of light and wisdom. The hue transcends the intellectual and reaches up into the realm of intuition, high spirituality, and intelligence."		Bustanoby		
GREEN	"The eye experiences a distinctly grateful impression from this color. If the two elementary colors (yellow and blue) are mixed in perfect equality so that neither predominates, the eye and the mind repose on the result of this junction as upon a simple color. The beholder has neither the wish nor the power to imagine a state beyond it."		Goethe	the hope of eternal life	growth hope

	positive associations	negative associations	writer	Catholic	heraldic
GREEN cont.	quieting, refreshing, peaceful, nascent	ghastliness, disease, terror, guilt	Birren		
	restful, freshness, faith, immortality, contemplation	immaturity	Graves		
	cool, refreshing, relaxing, healing, rejuvenating	jealousy, envy, self-ishness	Bustanoby		
	"Blue and green are the colours of the heavens, the sea, the fruit-ful plain, the shadow of the Southern noon, the evening, the remote mountains. They are essentially atmospheric and not substantial co-lours. They are cold, they disembody and they evoke impressions of distance and boundlessness. And for this reason an atmospheric blue-green is the space-creating element throughout the history of our perspective oil-painting... Blue and green are transcendent, spiritual, non-sensuous colours."		Spengler		
BLUE	"a stimulating negation," "a kind of contradiction between ex-citement and repose"		Goethe	piety sincerity	
	cool, serene, passive, tranquil		Graves		
	the spiritual color, inspires peace and introspection; the most soothing, sub-duing and cooling color	cold, indifferent, depressing ("the blues")	Bustanoby		
VIOLET	dignified, mystic	pompous, mournful, lone-liness, desperation	Birren	affliction melancholy	royalty rank
	dignified, elevating, oneness with the spirit, refined, mystery	penance, melancholy	Bustanoby		
	the color of the unconscious, the secret; threatening, of catastrophy (dark violet)	can be reassuring or or heavenly love (light violet)	Itten		

ASSERTIONS REGARDING COLOR PREFERENCES (not to be taken too seriously)

****

GOETHE: "Colors, as connected with particular frames of mind, are again a consequence of peculiar character and circumstances. Lively nations, the French for instance, love intense colors, especially on the active side; sedate nations, like the English and Germans, wear straw-colored or leather-colored yellow accompanied with dark blue. Nations aiming at dignity of appearance, the Spaniards and Italians for instance, suffer the red color of their mantles to incline to the passive side... The female sex in youth is attached to rose color and sea-green, in age to violet and dark green. The fair-haired prefer violet, as opposed to light yellow, the brunettes, blue, as opposed to yellow-red..." (For Goethe, 'passive' referred to the warm, light colors-- yellow-red, red-yellow and yellow, while 'active' referred to the dark, cool colors--blue-red, red-blue and blue.)

ITTEN: "Light-haired people with blue eyes and pink complexion generally prefer pure colors... Depending on the individual's vitality, the colors preferred may be more or less pale or more or less radiant. Quite different preferences are found in people with black hair, dark complexion and dark-brown eyes. For them, black plays an important role in (preferred) harmonies, and (they prefer) the pure colors mixed with black..."

SCHACHTEL: "Rorschach considered the preference for blue and green with avoidance of red as a peculiarity of people who are controlling their affects. From the context of this remark it is clear that he did not mean a free and easy, 'natural' control, but an outspoken one, requiring some degree of energy, although not necessarily conscious energy. These people seem to sense some danger in the red and think it better to stay away from it. That 'controlled' affectivity may be expressed in the preference for green color, finds a culturally interesting confirmation in Havelock Ellis' thesis that the preference for green developed in English literature with the rise of Puritanism in the Seventeenth century... The co-appearance of blue and green as preferred by the affect-controlling group is easily understood if the nature of these colors is considered. Blue draws one into the distance, perhaps a greenish blue even more so..."

ASSERTIONS REGARDING CORRESPONDENCES BETWEEN MUSIC AND COLOR
****

	notes according to Newton	relationships between color and musical instruments according to:		
		Oswald Spengler, THE DECLINE OF THE WEST	Albert Lavignac, MUSIC AND MUSICIANS (cited by Graves)	Christopher Ward (cited by Birren)
RED	C	"Yellow and red... colours of nearness, the <u>popular</u> colours, are associated with the brass timber, the effect of which is corporeal often to the point of vulgarity."	crimson: trumpets, trombones ordinary red: cornet	bugle call
ORANGE	D		trumpets and horns	brass
YELLOW	E		horn	piping
BROWN		"The strings in the Orchestra represent, as a class, the colours of the distance. The bluish-green of Watteau is found already in the Neopolitan bel canto of about 1700... The woodwind, too, calls up illumined distances."	bassoon	bass
GREEN	F		oboe	woodwind
BLUE	G		flute	
INDIGO	A			
VIOLET	B		cor anglais	oboe
BLACK			percussion instruments	
BLACK & WHITE			piano	

NB. Birren also cites Beethoven as describing B minor as "the black key," and Rimsky-Korsakoff as experiencing sunlight as C major and F sharp as strawberry red. (No sources are given.)

ASSERTIONS REGARDING FORMS WHICH CORRESPOND TO COLORS (to be taken with a grain of salt)
****

	according to ITTEN	according to BIRREN
RED	"The square corresponds to red as the color of matter. Red's weight and opacity fit the square's static and heavy form."	"Red suggests the square or cube. It is hot, dry, and opaque in quality. Being advanced in character, it holds strong attraction and appears solid and substantial... sharply focused by the eye, it lends itself to structural planes and sharp angles."
ORANGE		"Orange suggests the form of the rectangle. It is less earthly than red and more tinged with incandescence. Optically it produces a sharp image, is clearly focused by the eye, and lends itself to fine angles and details."
YELLOW	"The triangle symbolizes thought and the color equivalent of its weightless quality is radiant yellow."	"Yellow is abstractly related to the inverted triangle or pyramid. It is the color of highest visibility in the spectrum and therefore pointed and sharp. However, it is more celestial than worldly and it lacks substance and weight."
GREEN		"Green suggests the form of the hexagon or icosahedron. It is cool, fresh and soft. Because it is not sharply focused by the eye, it does not lend itself to much angularity."
BLUE	"the circle calls forth a feeling of relaxation and continuous movement.. symbolizes spirit gathered in itself.. corresponds to blue."	"Blue suggests the form of the circle or sphere. It is cold, wet, transparent, celestial. It is retiring in quality and creates a blurred image on the retina. Blue objects seen at a distance are never sharp to the eye."
PURPLE or VIOLET		"Purple suggests the form of the oval. It is soft, flowing, and cannot be clearly focused. Unlike blue, however, it seems to cling more closely to the earth."

****

"...no diamond shows colour so pure as a dewdrop; the ruby is like the pink of an ill-dyed and half-washed-out print, compared to the dianthus; and the carbuncle is usually quite dead unless set with a foil, and even then is not prettier than the seed of a pomegranate. The opal is, however, an exception. When pure and uncut in its native rock, it presents the most lovely colours that can be seen in the world, except those of clouds.

We have thus in nature, chiefly obtained by crystalline conditions, a series of groups of entirely delicious hues; and it is one of the best signs that the bodily system is in a healthy state when we can see these clearly in their most delicate tints, and enjoy them fully and simply, with the kind of enjoyment that children have in eating sweet things."

****

SPREADING. This is one of the striking examples used by Gombrich. Despite appearances to the contrary, the blue color is uniform throughout the pattern. (See page 12 above.)

GOLDSTEIN ON THE FUNCTIONS OF COLOR IN PAINTING
****

NB. Goldstein's typology may seem somewhat rudimentary. It is, however, the ONLY attempt to describe the range of functions fulfilled by color, found in any of the books listed in the bibliography on pages 31-32. In this respect, it is an admirable pioneering effort in an area that has been sorely neglected.

1. DESCRIPTIVE: "...color can describe a subject's various hues, its particular reds, blues, etc., and the tints and shades of hues, the lighter and darker states of colors resulting from light rays playing upon the subject's forms. This descriptive function is color's most simple and straightforward role: the chair is light green, the blouse is dark blue, etc. When color is limited to descriptive duties, forms, when modeled, are generally treated monochromatically..."

2. STRUCTURAL/SPATIAL: "A second important function of color is in the building of form and space. Because in certain ordered arrangements various colors will appear to advance while others will seem to recede, color can play an active and even dominant role in forming a volume's structure and its spatial 'container'... The artist who regards color as a primary means of realizing form and space rather than as only an adjunct to it is usually less concerned with a subject's surface character--its tactile or textural nature--but seeks instead to comprehend its underlying structural and dynamic nature."

3. CREATING TENSIONS, MOVEMENT, ENERGY: "to provide patterns of hue and intensity...(which) move or pulsate upon the picture-plane in ways quite independent of the descriptive or structural roles of color. One such basis for abstract color-play is the relational play of hues... " "...any changes in a color's hue, value, or intensity suggests movement--energy. Just as we sense motion when a group of lines or shapes shows gradually decreasing intervals, or undergoes a change in size or configuration, or when a sequence of tones moves from light to dark, so do we sense a moving energy in a gradual shift from say, yellow ochre to cadmium yellow..."

4. EXPRESSIVE/EVOKING MOOD: Goldstein refers to the "strong emotive powers" and "expressive force" of color, and "the psychological mood of a painting's total color-character." "Because the expressive force of color is somewhat autonomous, highly abstract and non-objective works can evince all manner of provocative or pleasant moods through its use."

SOME LANDMARKS IN THE HISTORY OF COLOR THEORY
****

ARISTOTLE "Sense and the Sensible" ca 350 BC	"Aristotle had proposed that all colors are derived from mixtures of black and white... The Aristotelian view held that white light is the purest light, and when light appears colored it has been contaminated" (Williamson & Cummins). "Aristotle realized that light is necessary for color, and that ordinary objects appear colored only because they absorb light. The Greeks lacked a word for absorption, so Aristotle used the word for 'contamination'. Aristotle taught that material objects impose blackness on the white light that falls upon them and that different colors are produced when various objects impose different kinds of blackness on the white light" (SCIENCE OF COLOR).
NEWTON Optick 1666	"According to Newton all colors were contained in white light... Being something of a mystic as well as a scientist, Newton chose seven principal colors and allied them to the proverbial seven spheres or planets and to the seven notes of the diatonic scale in music... Although the spectrum ran in a straight band from red to violet, Newton did the ingenious thing of twisting it into a circle. In the physical sense, red and violet were opposite. Visually, however, they bore resemblance. The connecting link was purple: 'The colour compounded shall not be any of the prismatick Colours, but of a purple inclining to red and violet" (Birren). "(Newton's) notion that passing white light through a glass prism will reveal differently colored components of the original light was not readily accepted... The ideas of Aristotle were still widely viewed as authoritative" (Williamson & Cummins). "...it is manifest, that if the Sun's Light consisted of but one sort of Rays, there would be but one Colour in the whole World, nor would it be possible to produce any new Colour by reflexions or Refractions, and by consequence that the variety of Colours depends upon the composition of light" (Newton, quoted in SCIENCE OF COLOR).

LE BLON Traité du Coloris 1756	First described the three substitutive primaries: "Painting can represent all visible objects with three colors, namely Yellow, Red and Blue; for all the other colors can be produced from these three, which I call primary colors (couleurs primitives)" (Le Blon, cited by Birren).
THOMAS YOUNG 1802	"Through a series of experiments he demonstrated that a wide range of the colors we know can be reproduced by superimposing blue, green and red lights in proper proportion. This fact suggests that the human visual system has analogous characteristics, and Young proposed that the eye has three different types of color receptors that are selectively sensitive to light in these three regions of the spectrum" (Williamson & Cummins).
GOETHE Farbenlehre 1810	"Not really understanding Newton he reverted to an Aristotelian approach and dealt in vague poetic terms that do not stand up to careful and objective scrutiny. Yet his book is important, for its careful observations showing the highly complex relationship between physical stimulus and perception served as a forerunner of the modern field of perceptual psychology... (Goethe) supposed that white light has to be mixed with darkness to produce color. He argued for the unity and indivisibility of light and contemptuously referred to Newton's demonstrations as 'the epoch of a decomposed ray of light'" (Williamson & Cummins). "Goethe's theory of the origin of the spectrum ISN'T a theory of its origin that has proved unsatisfactory; it is really not a theory at all. NOTHING can be predicted by means of it..." (Wittgenstein, III §125).
CHEVREUL "De la loi du contraste.." 1839	Director of the dye house at the Gobelins tapestry works outside Paris, Chevreul studied the contrast effects of color more systematically than anyone had before. A number of French painters, including Delacroix, Pissarro and Signac, took an interest in his work.

JAMES CLERK MAXWELL ca 1860	"He showed how each color could be specified by the amounts of three standard red, green and blue lights that must be added to reproduce the color of interest. He thereby initiated the quantitative science of colorimetry... His experiments with spinning discs on which are mounted adjustable lengths of colored paper enabled him to explore quantitatively the color mixing laws" (Williamson & Cummins).

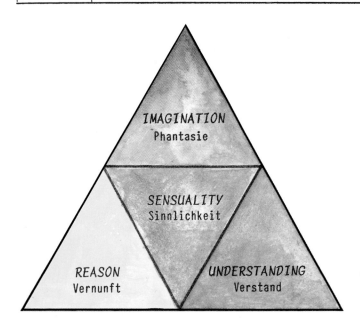

Reconstruction of Goethe's pyramid showing the 'soul power' of the colors. The qualities assigned here to the colors bear no apparent relationship to Goethe's characterization of the colors in §765-802 of his FARBENLEHRE (cited in part on pages 20-22 above.)

BIBLIOGRAPHY

****

Agoston, G.A. COLOR THEORY AND ITS APPLICATION IN ART AND DESIGN. Berlin: Springer, 1979.

Albers, Josef. INTERACTION OF COLOR. New Haven: Yale University Press, 1971; orig. pub. 1963.

Arnheim, Rudolf. ART AND VISUAL PERCEPTION. A PSYCHOLOGY OF THE CREATIVE EYE. Berkeley & L.A.: Univ. of California Press, 1969; orig. pub. 1954.

Bang, Jens Peter. FARVELÆRE. København: Nyt Nordisk Forlag, 1957.

Birren, Faber. COLOR PSYCHOLOGY AND COLOR THERAPY. Secaucus: Citadel, 1961; orig. pub. 1950.

Birren, Faber. PRINCIPLES OF COLOR. A REVIEW OF PAST TRADITIONS AND MODERN THEORIES OF COLOR HARMONY. New York: Van Nostrand Reinhold, 1969.

Bustanoby, J. H. PRINCIPLES OF COLOR AND COLOR MIXING. New York: McGraw-Hill, 1947.

Carpenter, James M. COLOR IN ART. Cambridge: Harvard University, 1974.

Chevreul, M. E. THE PRINCIPLES OF HARMONY AND CONTRAST OF COLORS. New York: Reinhold, 1967; trans. of DE LA LOI DU CONTRASTE SIMULTANÉ DES COULEURS, 1839.

Dantzig, M. M. van. PICTOLOGY. Leiden: Brill, 1973.

Ehrenzweig, Anton. THE HIDDEN ORDER OF ART. London: Paladin, 1970; orig. pub. 1967.

Evans, Ralph M. THE PERCEPTION OF COLOR. New York: John Wiley & Sons, 1974.

GOETHE'S COLOR THEORY. London: Studio Vista, 1971.

Goldstein, Nathan. PAINTING. VISUAL AND TECHNICAL FUNDAMENTALS. Englewood Cliffs: Prentice-Hall, 1979.

Gombrich, E. H. ART AND ILLUSION. A STUDY IN THE PSYCHOLOGY OF PICTORIAL REPRESENTATION. London: Phaidon, 1962; orig. pub. 1959.

Gotfredsen, Lise. BILLEDETS FORMSPROG. Aarhus: 1978.

Graves, Maitland. COLOR FUNDAMENTALS. New York: McGraw-Hill, 1952.

Hansen, William. DEN ELEMENTÆRE FARVELÆRE. København: Høst & Søns Forlag, 1967.

Hiler, Hilaire. NOTES ON THE TECHNIQUE OF PAINTING. London: Faber & Faber, 1934.

Itten, Johannes. DESIGN AND FORM. THE BASIC COURSE AT THE BAUHAUS. New York: Reinhold, 1965; trans. of MEIN VORKURS AM BAUHAUS' GESTALTUNGS- UND FORMENLEHRE, Otto Maier Verlag, 1963.

Itten, Johannes. FARVEKUNSTENS ELEMENTER. København: Borgen, 1977; trans. of KUNST DER FARBE, Otto Maier Verlag, 1961.

Jacobson, Egbert. BASIC COLOR. Chicago: Paul Theobald, 1948.

Kornerup, Andreas. OM OPFATTELSE AF FARVER. København: Sadolin og Holmblad, 1967.

Kornerup, Andreas and Johan Henrik Wanscher. FARVER
I FARVER. København: Politikens Forlag, 1974.

Lehmann, Alfred. FARVERNES ELEMENTÆRE ÆSTHETIK.
København: Rudolf Klein, 1884.

Marx, Ellen. THE CONTRAST OF COLORS. New York: Van
Nostrand Reinhold, 1973.

Møller, Hans-Jacob. DETERMINATIONS INTERNATIONALES
DES COULEURS. København: A. Rosenberg, 1910.

Runge, Ph. Otto. FARBEN-KUGEL / FARVEKUGLE. København:
Skolen for Kunstpædagogik, 1973; orig. pub. 1810.

Ruskin, John. THE ELEMENTS OF DRAWING. London: Black-
friars, n.d. (1857); LECTURES ON ART. London: George
Allen, 1898.

Schachtel, Ernest G. "On color and affect," PSYCHIATRY
vol 6, November 1943, pp. 393-409.

Silfverberg, Erik. FARVELÆRE. København: Den grafiske
Højskole, 1976.

Spengler, Oswald. THE DECLINE OF THE WEST. New York:
Knopf, 1962; trans. of DER UNTERGANG DES ABENLANDS,
1922.

Williamson, Samuel J. and Herman Z. Cummins. LIGHT AND
COLOR IN NATURE AND ART. New York: Wiley, 1983.

Wittgenstein, Ludwig. REMARKS ON COLOR / BEMERKUNGEN
ÜBER DIE FARBEN. Oxford: Blackwell, 1977.

THE SCIENCE OF COLOR. Committee on Colorimetry, Optical
Society of America. New York: Crowell, 1953.

DANISH TERMS FOR THE ATTRIBUTES OF COLOR
****

ENGLISH	DANISH
hue	kulør, farvetone
saturation (or chroma)	mætning, mættethed ; tæthed ; kulørthed
brightness (or value)	skyggegrad; sorthed; mørkhed/lyshed
brilliance (saturation + brightness)	valør (NB. valør ≠ value)
chromaticity (hue + saturation)	kromaticitet